RAPTUS

ALSO BY JOANNA KLINK

CIRCADIAN
THEY ARE SLEEPING

RAPTUS

Joanna Klink

PENGUIN POETS

PENGUIN BOOKS

Published by the Penguin Group
Penguin Group (USA) Inc., 375 Hudson Street,
New York, New York 10014, U.S.A.
Penguin Group (Canada), 90 Eglinton Avenue East, Suite 700, Toronto,
Ontario, Canada M4P 2Y3 (a division of Pearson Penguin Canada Inc.)
Penguin Books Ltd, 80 Strand, London WC2R 0RL, England
Penguin Ireland, 25 St Stephen's Green, Dublin 2,
Ireland (a division of Penguin Books Ltd)
Penguin Group (Australia), 250 Camberwell Road, Camberwell,
Victoria 3124, Australia (a division of Pearson Australia Group Pty Ltd)
Penguin Books India Pvt Ltd, 11 Community Centre,
Panchsheel Park, New Delhi – 110 017, India
Penguin Group (NZ), 67 Apollo Drive, Rosedale, North Shore 0632,
New Zealand (a division of Pearson New Zealand Ltd)
Penguin Books (South Africa) (Pty) Ltd, 24 Sturdee Avenue,
Rosebank, Johannesburg 2196, South Africa

Penguin Books Ltd, Registered Offices:
80 Strand, London WC2R 0RL, England

First published in Penguin Books 2010

10 9 8 7 6 5 4 3 2 1

Page vii constitutes an extension of this copyright page.

LIBRARY OF CONGRESS CATALOGING IN PUBLICATION DATA
Klink, Joanna, date.
Raptus / Joanna Klink.
    p. cm. — (Penguin poets)
ISBN 978-0-14-311772-8
I. Title.
PS3561.L5R37 2010
811'.6—dc22   2010008246

Printed in the United States of America
Set in ITC Galliard • Designed by Elke Sigal

for Deborah Busch and Patrick Hutchins

ACKNOWLEDGMENTS

Some of these poems have appeared under different titles, in other forms. *Wonder of Birds* was printed as a chapbook by Hand Held Editions.

What Is (War) is reprinted from LONG JOURNEY: CONTEMPORARY NORTHWEST POETS, edited by David Biespiel (Oregon State University Press, 2006).

AT LENGTH   *Sorting, Wonder of Birds*

BLACK WARRIOR REVIEW   *Junkyard*

BOSTON REVIEW   *Wayfaring*

CHICAGO REVIEW   *The Radiant*

COLUMBIA: A JOURNAL OF LITERATURE & ART   *Safekeeping*

DENVER QUARTERLY   *Paraphrase of Several Guesses, What Is (War)*

GULF COAST   *Some Feel Rain*

HARVARD DIVINITY BULLETIN   *The Graves*

H.O.W. JOURNAL   *Aftermaths and Wish-clouds, Half Omen Half Hope*

JUBILAT   *Poetry*

MASSACHUSETTS REVIEW   *Raptus*

OPEN CITY   *Lodestar*

POETRY NORTHWEST   *My Enemy*

Grateful acknowledgment to The University of Montana, Harvard University, and The MacDowell Colony.

To my family my love.

Ken White, thank you.

Thank you Paul Slovak, Prageeta Sharma, John D'Agata, Lois Welch, Jerry Fetz, Honor Moore, Youna Kwak, Saul Melman, Dorothy Wang, Caroline Woolard, Leni Zumas, and Jonathan Farmer.

Raptus (1) A state of rapture or furor. Also: an instance of this; a fit of intense emotion. (2) A seizure; a sudden or acute attack (as in *a raptus of the blood, Impulsive Raptus,* or *Raptus Nervorum*). (3) From *rapio:* A carrying-off by force. (4) A state of spiritual rapture marked by anesthesia. (5) A pathological paroxysm of activity giving vent to impulse or tension (as in an act of violence).

CONTENTS

Love the World—and stay inside it.

Charles Olson, *The Maximus Poems*, III

RAPTUS

SOME FEEL RAIN

Some feel rain. Some feel the beetle startle
in its ghost-part when the bark
slips. Some feel musk. Asleep against
each other in the whiskey dark, scarcely there.
When it falls apart, some feel the moondark air
drop its motes to the patch-thick slopes of
snow. Tiny blinkings of ice from the oak,
a boot-beat that comes and goes, the line of prayer
you can follow from the dusking wind to the snowy owl
it carries. Some feel sunlight
well up in blood-vessels below the skin
and wish there had been less to lose.
Knowing how it could have been, pale maples
drowsing like a second sleep above our temperaments.
Do I imagine there is any place so safe it can't be
snapped? Some feel the rivers shift,
blue veins through soil, as if the smokestacks were a long
dream of exhalation. The lynx lets its paws
skim the ground in snow and showers.
The wildflowers scatter in warm tints until
the second they are plucked. You can wait
to scrape the ankle-burrs, you can wait until Mercury
the early star underdraws the night and its blackest
districts. And wonder. Why others feel
through coal-thick night that deeply colored garnet
star. Why sparring and pins are all you have.
Why the earth cannot make its way towards you.

POETRY

It left in the wind, it returned in the air.
I opened wide my door to it.

I shuttered all the rooms to block out
sunlight. It left at midnight.

It seemed to me there were birds
in that dark. I locked all the exits—

it returned in the fissures, the errors,
the marooned sulking thoughts.

What in the meantime happened
was nothing. Requiring no company,

plummeted into its own blood-
blackness. We were careless. It left

at the green summer of dawn.
Pulled us from a dream—no one

heard it. It gave every reason,
declared itself broken, gathered into

a cracked leather satchel its alarm clock
and books. I have come to tell you

there are no new stars. If you tense
against me there is history—I open

my body to it. Everyone at times
gets too close. But when I backed

into that delirium, unearthed
its warm flesh—it left. It left

with the heat from the stones and even
the dusk felt oppressive.

But when I rooted into your chest
and slept in a blue curve by

your thigh it returned. Felt
something shift in your skull—

no one saw it. Every day we must
live this. If you vanish

you are still there. Smoke,
do your laundry—one still has dignity—

no one has noticed. What good
is a conversation in darkness that

isn't raw. Requiring no company
we stayed there. Inseparable

loneliness. It left, it raged,
it wished to be quit of all pain—

who can blame it? I loved it—
I opened my body to it. It tore

through my cells, blistered my eyes—
I took it into my arms told it

please. I held it to my throat un-
abashed. You are here to explain this

in torrents—a rain that never comes.
It left in the wind, it spoke as it turned,

it carried me nowhere. Pulling me
close to its cheek. Even now as it goes.

SORTING

That day in June—we heard the echo of a meadowlark.

Let go the meadowlark and the valley in which its song
        repeated itself and the valley in which its song unfolded.

Let go the dream of such clear sound.

Let go the walks, dinners, drinks, talks, senses of beginnings, let go
        the beginnings, we will never begin again.

Let go the still gray sky. It has propped us up long enough.

Let go the nights.

Let go the voice that answered me in earnest in all things I find
        I can no longer imagine it.

Imagine the rents in the driveway cement from the rain that pooled
        and stayed and the way the cement buckled wildly in the years that followed
        and the years that followed in which no one came to the door.

You came to the door and said my name and the whole weathered mess
        glowed beneath hanging clouds and weeds
        grew in blunt stalks from the cracks.

Who would you change for?

The maples change more in an hour of wind than we change.

The aspens shatter light I have felt the leaves in their wind-glittering
        strangeness. Let go

the town and its dry river paths the white bellies of the swallows
          under the bridge flashing in the last minutes of dusk and I knew I could not
          continue as I had been nor did I sense a course.

Who are your friends.

What do you care for.

What would you give up if you could give up
          anything. When were you afraid there is no extreme need that is not
                    warped by fear. What does the world

          require of you have you loved the time you have spent here.
                    Was it because of the people with you. Or that the silence

was never silence it was always the fan's white noise in the window
          at night and below that the new rain on the grass
          and below that the grass as it bends under water
          and night buried under water and the town
          at night under rain and grateful for rain in this dry season.

*

There and not there like the wind in the yard.

There and not there in a smile that is not
          itself but a thought in a far country and a brush
                    of the shoulder that in a single minute means

everything. Everything you have said in support and questioned.
          In support of love that unfolds where one least
                    imagines it for example a year of endings.

A white shirt. A shoelace a razor. A pacing in the hallways at night
       like the lines of bicycles fanning across flat green fields.

The shadow of an airplane over the field or that shadow
       as it ripples over a building through the thick windless
       heat. Are you paying attention
       to what passes through you.

                Through you
I came to see a better life but cannot
account for why I have not always
       lived it.

A polite vagueness in the *Goodbye!* and *Good luck!*

Goodbye to the laughter I love I did not keep it close enough.

Goodbye to the mind that moves along walls and roads its un-
       ceasing spirit I wish I were always in its path.

To the boys playing soccer at five in the leafy park goodbye
       their gamesmanship goodbye
              goodbye to the gravel they scattered the ground
              they scuffed the houses they return to, may they always have homes.

Goodbye to the buses and the poppies that flew
            past us behind bus-windows in deep red-orange-dotted-
      smudges and the edgeless fields where you
          walked when I wasn't
          there, with you, in your head,
          where you walked, were you
          alone, were there
          fields, how alone
          were you. How

alone can anyone
stand to be. Any one of us might be
            tapped any one led away when that day
                    comes will you be
ready. Will you be prepared for what you
                    have not said.

Will you know what you love.

To have been alone together is to have been
            alone within an
            illusion. Step into a dream
            of life its tapwater shoes its
            coffee-cups paper-clips sheets the white light
that backs every curtain every room casually
            shared every question will you help me with this I will help you.

Step into a life that is not
            dreamed and try to say now if there are
            remnants of illusion.

Is what you say every day real.

Are the lesser estrangements
            deeper and if so how much can you bear and if not
            what will convince you.

Does the sparrow on the t.v. antenna convince you—it is there every day.

Every day the sun hits the red roofs of the village where you lived
            and every evening the swifts dive through the crooked stone streets
            chasing bugs we cannot see.

The birds rose
level with our torsos on the terrace and whistled
        their strong eerie whistle I heard it each morning a lone swift
                veering past our bedroom window.

The rains rose and fell through the winter
and the spring rose and the beating summer
        arrived. The birds arrived
        each night and often we took the stairs
to the terrace after dinner to watch their bodies
        drag drift-sharp a black-
        dotted moving cloud of themselves

and rise and spike and dive, each in its own private
        depth, sharp hap-
        hazard wing-splitting
                        rolls.

As if there were hundreds of separate skies.

*

So that nothing will ever again be for us what it was.

The long walk to the grocery store in noonwhite
        heat. The men standing immobile at boule, murmuring with the toss.

Constant church bells, the apple you set on the counter to eat,
        the shake of a head saying no. Let go
        the bistro the woman by the creek the disease.

Let go the young girl walking toward a building at the end of a city-
        sidewalk I see she is looking

toward someone there in the highest window her mother or a tutor
            watching her child and neither one of them needs to wave.

Had I been able to read the signs,
            had you been able to
            speak more clearly, had I
            noticed, not
            assumed, had you come to me
            in understanding linking need to
            need, had I
            heard you, had you
            spoken, I heard, as you
            said the words, the harder
            course, you
            insisted, nor
            have you always
            lived it, *persist*, and cannot any longer
            pass lightly over
            anything.

You came to me in understanding
and brought with you the need of a whole life,
            having for months looked elsewhere,
            the streets of the town after midnight, a nullity
                        in each livingroom's blue
                                    t.v., letters to others drought
in the mind in the neighborhood grass.

            Certain you would always be there.
            Certain you would follow.

The night's hours in talk and the paths our thoughts took
            together. The dust-choked house
and its unutterable shag carpet

or the blue house and all the passing cars stranded in its
        snowbanks bitter arguments
sweet reprieves the funny midwestern meals you cooked
mountain ash years without cigarettes
        heaps of sweaters dishes
        the fire in the kitchen the purple
        kitchen. The absurd red car your mother gave us
the books we wrote sentences we took out
        pencil in the margins your shrinking
        penmanship new shoes
        your smile the one that seizes at what's
real. The laundry the prosody. The refusals
            the constant generosities every desperate apology.

You have to hold it in mind all at once.

You have to need it enough.

*

If I let go what will be left. Too hard
        to sort each sorrow from each joy

        and why, instead of answering, we passed into silence.
        Clear, deep green, like a lake we've never been to

and stood at its blue edge-grass and felt
            nothing, like sunlight,
            as it moved across our faces.

And when it passed we didn't
            know. But we stayed.

SAFEKEEPING

My beloved, if it has come to this,
I will try to understand.
From the house we once lived in, from the room
that was yours, I hold my arms around myself
and hear you pacing, your thoughts stall and flee,
    cold snow in your lungs.
After so many years, if no change appears
there is either speech or action,
and you had never said *always* and I had never said
    completely. Only I knew.
In my dreams there are geese pulling south,
    burdened with cargo. I keep the radio close
and turn off the voices when I sense something near.
I no longer know whom to speak to.
I no longer know what to call you.
Lost-to-me, nested one, night owl.

WHAT IS (WAR)

And if all those who meet or even
hear of you become witness to what you are—

a white country of blight beneath the last snows of
spring. Could we remain quiet on earth

and bear it, the war we make inside
what is—it's a long time to be here, to be still,

to feel the rot inside *now*—bone-scrap, char, sheets of stars
at the edge of a field where we are once again

taken from ourselves. Could we remain here,
witness to grief, one last bright dire call-and-reply,

each birdsong or siren extinguished where some
trueness abides, some portion we have lost our right

to claim or know. It comes into any mind that would
perceive it, leaf-rot, speech-rot, the deliberate ribcage

of the deer, these abrupt chalk cliffs over which
the confused animals fling themselves, and you,

obscure, receive no response that is not suffered
as the days grow long and distortions

come to seem the natural course of things—
what trees whose creatures stray into space—

and they find they cannot land though the eyelid
struggles open—no answer, no resolution—

a window opened to the mute green world,
weedy and driftless, a wind drilling rain, dirt,

the parameters of uncertainty, of hope,
what we might be against what we have done,

bees crawling through the lips of the one
who would say *the earth turned into sour flesh*—

What strange rooms, what soundless movement of sky
over desert where the flesh again is beaten

and the emptiness extends itself while some old man
looks on, a raptor in waiting, the sand-field

around them blown thinly toward sun—no longer
ourselves in the afternoons, evenings,

weak, vague, clutched at the mouth—
because we did nothing, because we lost count.

PARAPHRASE OF SEVERAL GUESSES

Were there tares in the field?
    There were tares.

Were you wide-awake in the nicknames?
    In the nicknames, the walks, the curve of the moon.

So you were blind?
    Neither blind nor skilled.

Had you turned—
    With no one else would I have been willing to turn.

And you condemned him?
    He was my ice-light, slow star weaving toward me—
    a breeze a relief a hush-carried-home.

But you keep your own counsel.
    He keeps his own counsel.
    Insouciant, he'd say, unaware of my own comportment.

And you let him be?
    I did not let him be. Had I turned—

Had you turned—
    Earlier—and known—

What was gathering in the drawers
    And papers—

Vagaries—
    In the cupboards and nooks—

And he said the words?
        Parts of my self *scaled away*—

Neither sweet nor brutal.
        Neither steadfast nor free.

And the day-sleep?
        And the night-sleep.

And that deep content, that centering of help?
        Not doomed, not grievous.
        An ardor maddened and greened and full of form's light.

And the spites and faults?
        Called so in haste.

Called so in confusion.
        Having slept—

Having woken—
        Called so in carelessness—

Devastation—
        Called so in haste—

Like a children's game, where what hurts—
        Is destroyed—

What leaves you be—
        Blessed—

So the matchsticks flared then went dead—
        They did not go dead—

THE GRAVES

WHAT HAPPENED TO US
happened because we could not

stop. Needing belief in un-
inhabited wilderness,

in the twelve hours of
thunder over these hills.

Hope is a place
held for the unknown,

where you are beyond
anything I can say. Like animals

who form a quiet lake in the grass
long before scattering.

TO WARD OFF FEAR we could
listen for the burble of

the hermit thrush or else a
chickadee's three-dot-

note. Outwardly
you make safety in anonymity

but I know some part of you
opens as the day opens,

as the tomcat stretches then
marches lion-like through

the neighbor's wet weeds.
At times I have sensed no change

through the valley's haze
and felt the dozing stranglehold of

stillness. At times for years.
But the lines drawn in books

are the lines etched in cliffs
by the river and the swallows burrow

in them. River-cortège, cortège
of each living thing that unfolds—

a bird its wings, a forest,
an old man his eyes.

TO BE WORTHY of the dirt
that will one day surround my

body I say a blessing to
friendship, bicycles and

meals. Joy was never
our birthright. But it was an honor

to have loved you, to have woken
into you, to have been wide-

awake in you. I'm more
at ease now, when the day

goes astray as it does. Perhaps
the way to despair is based in

certainty. Just as inches
under this pocked river-surface

are fish that brighten with rain.
Are their scales gifts?

Their skeletons weights
rising and falling.

RAPTUS

The door to the past is a strange door. It swings open and things pass
through it, but they pass in one direction only. No man can return across
that threshold, though he can look down still and see the green light waver
in the weeds.

LOREN EISELEY

A door opens in the wilderness.
People cross through it—bloused women families

Acquaintances friends all the ones I have loved
Sleep-walkers night-walkers each dazed and shorn—

Streets aurous with ice, a snowfall scratched into
Moons—and everything I'd known—

Inside the bleak floating light of my lungs
In the capillaries of my eyes a blood

Glancing through the hatches—
If I said I would always be grateful

If I lied or touched with spite
If night is just a foamline of shadows

Though we were both lost—the door
Opening—the fear of being shown

Whole to the one who must *love you still*—
And stopped as if on a walk to say

Look at that and *what matters what really counts*
And I'll tell you everything if you promise I promise

I stood at the door and behind me heard
Snow-plows scrape against roads

At the center of night—*unknown to yourself*
And the word I said out-loud to no one

That meant *it was all to no purpose*
The word for *the desire inside destruction*

For everything that can never be brought back—
Loose snow blown hard to each bank

And the common reel of those who
To avoid one extreme rush toward its opposite—

Snow blasted to piles—and never opened up to
Anything that could reach me until you reached me—

Which hours belonged to us
When was I unknowingly alone

Why did you always return to walk here a path
Behind my closed eyes shedding salt

Dry snowfall and sticks—still were you here
With me I might say *The moon rose in the casement window*

The red-haired boy across the street has learned to ride his bike
There are still picnics there are fountains

And the world I am leaving behind says
One learns to see one learns to be kind—

I closed my eyes I closed my hands
I shut down the fields in my arms

The cattle on the plains veins ditches
Blue ravines a gray bird

Sailing through a poplar brake kids
Throwing snow I closed the last swinging juncos

Sheep wool caught on barbed wire I closed
Fumes and clear patches of sky I seized

The river the town I shut down
The hard muscles of sleep farmlands

Warming under midnight salt-lights scruff-pines
On the ridge animals scattering across slopes I closed

The smooth bone of evening a storm
On the hills white and noiseless spindled

Prairies where I was born I shut I seized
The clouds I closed in anger—fervor—*ardor*

MY ENEMY

My enemy. What is green and prickly-sick
or most yours—you live by it. Thoughtless
greed washing up and down your spine.
My knees barely hold me to the ground but I am
arborescing. I would not have known to
cull through all the hints and looks that now un-
clasp like padlocks. While I was holding on
to parts and tatters, you were famished, defiant,
compassing the possible consequences of
public subterfuge. Although you yawn,
each of us has been warped by separation.
The cause of night is not fathomless—
the pine-fields breathe when the sun draws off—
hoof-prints of deer fold under new snow.
Blindsided I held to him, not understanding what has now
opened in our midst. For me it is not common,
it is not comic. Take your time. You may yet find
that what we share rescinds itself with every hour,
a ghost who will not be encumbered by any
will not his own. Through the keyhole is a cut-out,
a miniature view of future colorless gauze.
I am all alone with you in that emptiness.

My enemy. You may still find a home there.
As every hour you fail to heed my presence
my eyes grow more alive. Once crumpled paper,
my body knits itself to skin and lines,
warm cord of my spine, and beyond my arms birds
motionless and quiet, rubies in the trees.
Your aggression, your estrangements are not
mine. Would the hill's red shadows
darken with that slight opiate sweetness,
would you understand the ropy blush of trees—
would you keep them company?
Can you understand company? I had lost my way.
Hardly visible by day, I stared all fall at that old
hopelessness. Evasions and tracks. Over years
I mistook the scree for slope, the feral hours for trifles.
Love so sprang at me I forgot there should be
more than that effusion, and as the music
withered I insisted it had strength.
As you have, as I have.
The way you hold something in you matters.

Nominal. You are not inscrutable.
A long drink of fog as March wells up from
clumps of mud. By April more will become clear,
more wind, more water loosened from packed snow.
Knotted up, at home in this beseeching season
where children in pink jackets strain against the
skyless gray, you find people bothersome.
Hubris. Ampersands and thumbtacks.
No talent thrives without sympathy.
No bookmark holds grievance for a spot.
But you are not without grace, for what you may
come to love, I too loved.
Do you ever follow those strands back to me,
whom you so effortlessly injured?
As he leans into you, you may starve less,
you whom I shall not reach or
speak to. Strange. The dirt seems no longer to tremble.
As if one had laid to rest a crucial desire
and said *I understand. It is yours.*

HALF OMEN HALF HOPE

When everything finally has been wrecked and further shipwrecked,
When their most ardent dream has been made hollow and unrecognizable,
They will feel inside their limbs the missing shade of blue that lingers
Against hills in the cooler hours before dark, and the moss at the foot of the forest
When green starts to leave it. What they take into their privacy (half of his embrace,
Her violence at play) are shadows of acts which have no farewells in them.
Moons unearth them. And when, in their separate dwellings, their bodies
Feel the next season come, they no longer have anyone to whom
To tell it. Clouds of reverie pass outside the window and a strange emptiness
Peers back in. If they love, it is solely to be adored, it is to scatter and gather
Themselves like hard seeds in a field made fallow by a fire someone years ago set.
In the quiet woods, from the highest trees, there is always something
Weightless falling; and he, who must realize that certain losses are irreparable,
Tells himself at night, before the darkest mirror, that vision keeps him whole.

On the verge of warm and simple sleep they tell themselves certain loves
Are like sheets of dark water, or ice forests, or husks of ships. To stop a thing
Such as this would be to halve a sound that travels out from a silent person's
Thoughts. The imprint they make on each other's bodies is worth any pain
They may have caused. Quiet falls around them. And when she reaches
For him the air greens like underwater light and the well-waters drop.
They will see again the shadows of insects.
They will touch the bark and feel each age of the tree fly undisturbed
Into them. If what is no longer present in them cannot be restored,
It can at least be offered. Through long bewildered dusks, stalks grow;
Rains fill and pass out of clouds; animals hover at the edges of fields
With eyes like black pools. For nothing cannot be transformed;
Pleasure and failure feed each other daily. Do not think any breeze,
Any grain of light, shall be withheld. All the stars will sail out for them.

THE RADIANT

What fell to the earth fell quickly,
flew into the forest with its lichen and salt.
    A flick of the conscience—
the night-tides hardly stirred.

Something that came from far within
and far off. In the lake beds, in the vegetable beds.
It was enough to loosen the bones of the moon.
I was living here, and you were living here—
    we had everything we needed.
At certain hours of the day there were clouds
in the leaves. Shelves of minerals—limestones,
gravestones, red stones pitched by tides.
Through the ground-smoke and tree-smoke it was enough
    to lie on the bed and it was enough
to open our hands from the wrist
and feel the gorgeous debris of ourselves, the far-off
drone of planes, that softest
    patch on the skull. Skull-skin, sea-skin,
skin-of-night, skin-of-grass. And the whales,
having traveled thousands of miles, and the elephant seals,
and the monarch flexing just now on the stem.
No matter what they tell you, something fell to the earth,
and the fire was blown sideways and each insect
    stopped. It was enough to get inside us
and our fat blue lakes and our dropsical features, our eyes
turning in their sockets like cool private gems.
Ice-gems, ruby-gems, gems-of-clay, gems-of-bone.
The hills came down and the kelp-forests swayed
    and we were rich, were warm-blooded.
And the civilians took refuge in the shed-flint,
    the sand, deliriums of quiet, as if

nothing had happened and they said
nothing has happened and the air touched the wicks.
   There were people: they all had names.
We wrote stories on the door and I wrote
poems on the door and it seemed as if we had taken
each measure against harm against sleep.
And when the rain finished, the deserts shone like mirrors
and you reached for me in the blazing dark.
   Who were we then? On the box-spring,
in the well-spring, spring-of-blood, spring-of-night?

No one to give our position away.

Far within and far off, a small pain
   grew into quiet, the color
of the many colors of flesh: flesh-heap,
wind-heap, heap-of-sand, heap-of-night.

When it is enough, we will bear it.
When it is enough, the dust-fields will bloom.
The sun's circadian trail will leave lines on the ground
   and when it is enough, we will crawl there.
Seasons, winds—moving along those sinews of dirt,
root-knots and tendons, it will be enough
they say, no matter what, nothing has changed—
   They all had names
and those names are passing through us,
hairclips and sweaters, shoelaces and charms,
raw quiet, bird-quiet, beaks and fine bones—
and you will not be released from the dream
   whose permanence is unease,
so that every story you tell from now on must include it,

and every body you love from now on must include it,
no matter what they tell you you know
    something has changed, everything that
never happened, everything that's now going so well,
like a square of light on the sea that held its force
    then dissolved, moon-bromide,
dusk-bromide, fish, soothing night,
and the trusses on the bridge will include it,
and the coastal scrub will include it—
tides of sunlight, delicate metals, tobacco and glue—
and we'll drive to work and drive home, sleepy,
    relieved, with that dark dry silence
in us, so that beyond all hindsight and guesswork
it will reach back and touch the first breath of the first animal
and it will reach forward to touch the fogs
    that have not yet formed, and on the sea-charts we'll mark it,
the skin-charts, the screens, all sutures and visitations,
people like ourselves who at certain hours of the day
    take refuge in coffee, cool interiors, in sheets—
the day-sleep, the night-sleep, sleep-of-fire, sleep-of-grass—
or at certain hours of the day
    simply stop—

We are homesick, we are sense-clipped, but what can we do?

We have brought ourselves here and now must
    bring ourselves back.
They were people first—this one, that one—
had children, laughed at supper, spoke sharply, felt fear.

And at dusk the boys played soccer—
    something far within and far off—
and if I knew their names I could not live,
and if I saw it in person I could not live,
and the close hours, the over-sweetness,
it would all be for naught—day-silks,
    blue-silks, silks-of-waves, silks-of-night—
and to act means to act again and again
and if you're lucky your life will be free of such grief
as touches those who light the first candle of evening
    in Baghdad—fire-swell, fire-braid, braid-of-skin, braid-of-night—
and if you're lucky you will still be undone by light snow,
and if you're lucky you'll know what to do—
I don't know what to do—so that no matter what they call it
    you will respond to it—they were people first—
like us, growing in beauty at the end of the day—
and when the truth appears it will be strange
and the fountains will rise and the gorges will stall,
the redwoods, the anchors, the fissures, the deeps—
heart-flint, wood-flint, wood-sorrel, wood-lark—
    so that what is desired is also *possible*,
far within and far off—along the train-tracks
and dream-tracks, the portals, the tides—

So that when it is enough, the sky will scatter.
When it is enough, men will see stars.

NOWHERE ARE WE SO CLOSE

Nowhere are we so close. Not in the train-car's
liquid window, the marshes that drop
back as I pass. Not in the first darkening of red
in the leaves against trunks blurred stick-
silver, as when once we felt we might return.
Not in November, when the herons in twos and threes
arch their wings over the sound, leaving no lash-marks
on the air that is their cadenza and companion,
and the streaming speeds at which the trees flare
and wilt, an old fury under-sung—they are not ghosts.
Nowhere are we so close as when the ground-clouds
wash the ankles of people in the borough,
at evening when I have arrived—nowhere
in the city where dawn is just a thought,
a small hold in my gut that still binds me to you.
What I am, each day, as I walk to the door.
To seek a firmament in the midst of bus-engines
and sirens, a canopy, peaceably, that spreads stars
in your lashes and joints and sends a lucent wind across
the placeless darknesses that are no dream backed by glass.
A nullity in that unconscious singing.
Spare and blood-warm. As when once
we leaned into one another. Understood.

AFTERMATHS AND WISH-CLOUDS
for S

Two arms dangle down
in a ghost forest.

> A beetle destroys the pine
> in increments, black
> vocalist. It should not be so

hard to understand. Even
a stranger, what you
seemed to me, stripped
bare. What entered

> your world once entered
> mine and crushed me.
> Does that mean we dovetail

only in despair, the velvet furs
wrapped around a center beating but still
star-dead and raw. Is it still

> such a long season we must
> pass through, its bone-wax and
> marrows, tufted

growth, decay, its predatory
fogs What you thought

you loved most must
disappear into you.

As you move, the trees sleeve
in moss and felt, each muscle

of her stomach rinsed into air.
Can you bear it?

No breath beyond the forest.
Just quiet.
The dream of what came.

JUNKYARD

You protect the loss, its
thousand materials. Midvein
when the smashed glass thins to

       dust. You protect the ruts and
       grooves, rose-hooked
       woods, slats, planks, entire

ghost forests that rise up in your
imagination of desire.
Should it be so hard

       to gather her hips, the cargo bed,
       back-stars that for years sprang
       up above the room's

smooth cove. Blue twilight
in the junkyard where even the wire

       nets are silk. If I called to you
       across the downpour of smoke

would you even hear me.
Would you protect the
orchard from moths or strip

       the wood and coat it with
       exquisite shellacs in your
       love below the hedge-clouds.

Having stored away such
riches, you press into the

      damages as if they could
      save you. Strangest
      creature, true

to what you
touched, could you
wrestle yourself enough

      to catch one voice
      sifting across a city.
      Or would you, in that dusty

motion, lifting your torso to
turn, lose the same blind
force that made you burn.

LODESTAR

A lodestar held lightly in the sky above a gray
page of snow. Someone speaks a word

and the boats are born to time, trailing out against the ice.
And we judge this valuable—weather undone across a field,

the boats soft black discs upon the whitening water.
And the heat that forms within our throats

as we stand and look out. Who are you, next to me?
To shine in unawareness like the ice at night on the field.

To say the only thing you want—boats below a lodestar
and in another country, beyond a gray wave of snow

where a girl sits in a chair, emerging from thought
or preparing a future. Seeds float through the air

beneath a fire maple—it is late in the day or it is
autumn. Someone brings me a newspaper

—it is you. Had I understood what portions
would be lost or made solid by the pressures of

one star rising each evening in winter,
one fire maple dropping a few leaves in the casual winds.

Further out, someone says a word into the summer air
and a bird emerges from the lawn's warm shadow,

a deep gray spread across the northern sea
where boats form a slow nomenclature of movement,

and everywhere we look out upon a darkness
whose scarcity we cannot comprehend—

seagulls resting against the liquid light, the fringe
of a crowd drawn, like us, to stare midway into sea,

into a field I have tried for so long to pull
free from—the slight glow

of our bodies in these rooms, a few words
that hold their sound across the stillness of hours.

You feel a star in its private heat above a field,
a woman curled into sleep or walking among the long

bars of shadow-trees through which pour shining
coins. To each belong the corrections of light,

suffering that shall not heal, the singing that lifts
—washed, unwinged—from a small boat at sea.

CARGOS, ISLANDS, SHORES

Didn't I try hard enough   Weren't the evenings
strange   slipping out the back door

dry smell of pines   laid across the night air the sky
a dome of doves   Weren't the days strange

sheer cotton dress an oversized sweater
you slipped   into books   Roads fanned out

gravel scrawlings   rich futures
a haven an island   charcoal sand its

snow-shaped cargos   And wood animals
flickering through trees   in the moon-white surplus

Why is night   your terrain   throat of stars
Didn't I try   Rummaging around the nightstand

exhausted by solitude   waves inking the rocks
you were out walking   pain   barely held back by skin

The spruce   is a wish   Suppose suppose
the road had slipped unbeknownst

into a tract of firs   pools   night-insects skittish
instruments of perception you had a knack

for smiling   There was never wind
never a single clear   moment of separation

you walked   for weeks as I slept
scrawlings on water beating wings

After all   it was years of our lives
That road seems landless   red-turquoise

collapsed roof of a barn   in the garden soft nets
to hold them back   whole cartographies

where the deer have stepped   seeds of rain
Didn't you   want it more

my body you sensed   flurries
as black moths   rearrange themselves against the glass

when the light-source   shifts
Ruin   sleep   shadows of ferns

Washed up   on a shore the 77 months
that are inside me   as my life now continues

slipping   into another hot bath cavalier
to think it would work itself out   a ringing

against the waves   cold ribbons of fish
And want to go home

if only we knew what that meant
Weren't we foolish   Weren't we wise

to part ways the aspen   in the backyard
its metallic leaves   is flourishing   Sparks

fly up where you step   blazing atmospheres
storms   tearducts   Lest we think

the world has hardened we do not   harden
Sleepwalker   suppose   there are other loves

velvet-wet   night on the tarmac
I will always adore you   So long

WAYFARING

I would remain by night with you
who, having held me once, wrapped everything I knew
into my sleeping body's hold and held fast and stayed.
You shuttled in sleep against me and away, not sleeping,
beached and exhausted by wine and rushes from
another life whose body my body meant to alter.
But I am wayfaring and recently wrecked;
I understand the cost of pulling free from what once loved you.
I would remain by night with you, if the night is clear enough
to see by, and the wind light enough to draw the stars
in the skin's skies open, and the waves you sensed
through the dress in the wind are real, and only mine.

IF YOU WAKE

If you wake with me in the dark,
your body a breadth of waves
against the outstretched ocean.
Where my breath unmoored, you brooded and held,
slowing the chords of hard tides.
And broke, in that night-sailing-motion,
a sharp pool of sun against my shoulders.
And the light traveled back and forth, just audible, between us.

AND I WOKE

And I woke and felt you near me,
and you seemed as real as the waves
that had moved through us.
And touched you, rooted in sleep,
dark earth-warmth drawn up into skin.
And I spoke these words to you, since you were nearest.
And you heard, since you were there.

AERIAL

Scissors   embers   misnomers   Are you this

loneliness of hands   Do you burrow past kindness

Are you no less than a cell dividing no more   than an arboretum

Who has visited you   Who has kept your dark eyes in thrall

Is there a clear sound   threading through   What you want

What you say   What you do   Do you know what you are losing

when the dusk seals off the center of things   in the parks

Hour of dismissal   Nobody stops to sit   as they did during day

I am listening   to the peace that gathers   in the husky throats of

mourning doves   the children   with no need of goods

They told us what our eyes feel   being outside is enough

The moon moves quickly   The years   could shut us out

There is an ache in the lungs   so deep   it can't be heard

A floating-inward   rush of air   Are you rosin   wax

Are you alizarin-crimson   the spiraling glitters of pelicans

over the cone marsh the threshold   at which change becomes

unstoppable   We are traveling   through the unmanifest dark

and have only our skin   to glide by   I will vouch for you

when you make a place for me   in the city of soft gray-bodied trees

If I have a wish   it is to find you   where I find poetry

Do you ever   close your eyes in full sunlight   Here close your eyes

You are everything   that has not yet been lost

WONDER OF BIRDS

If it is possible to touch the hour,
the burr, that whole up-
ended half-decade we spent
wondering about each other—
you slumped on your kitchen floor arms crossed arguments
stockpiled. Will we thieve or be brave?

Today, where the wind is full of snow
that will not fall, brown leaves
curled against the blanched grass,
I suspect there are no gardens in you.
You suspect I am brimming with vast shadows,
the way the mud and sky
are brimming with snow.

Winds chafe the maples and somewhere
an animal huddles under woodland trash.

Will it be now, or later?

Will it be now?

. . . . .

When the diagnosis came he said, in his head,
anything to be free from harm.

I too said *anything*.

The lesions hooked down, flew into the nerves,
numbing the left hand and left foot,
blood-threads scorched with orchids, skulls,
white forest fires, your future
fisted and refisted in the neurologist's dusky
speech. You will never be alone.
You will walk the hallways in radiator heat and summer heat,
and the blackboards will be coated with your tiny letters
and the portals of minds will open and close, open and close.
Waterlogged, the cemetery by the highway
sinks further into itself as the violet dirt
darkens. Everything
has changed. The way,
from a tree, a whole curve of birds
issues from one startled call.

· · · · ·

We understood we were afraid.
I understood the promise I made in that moment
was binding.
You felt for a moment I was with you—
    I was with you.

It stayed with me in the lamp dusk, blue trees and fields,
months of solitude, an occasional gift we exchanged,
the plans you made without hope.

I give my hands hopelessly
in the blur of this mid-winter mid-afternoon hour,
mud wicking from cement and wet weeds,
a broom to brush the pooled
sidewalk-ice away.
Something nearby moves just
beyond us. The trees raw from wind
as shadows of birds fly out.

. . . . .

Are you disenthralled?

Avert your eyes if you can.

Have a drink have a smoke.

Spend a month on a kitchen floor—

Stop reading the paper.

You can have a drink—

You can go buy a drink.

Slip outside and smoke.

Find someone and lean back.

Recede, withdraw—

Withdraw—

Don't be afraid—

. . . . .

I didn't think the world *desired* us.
I never thought that when winter ends in February
the seasons might be *lying*.

What can move from your throat
now that some violence has
pulled us apart?

Was it mine?

When a person throws herself backwards
off a ledge in a small town in the mountains,
late gold-warm brick, a few scraps of weeds,
not high enough to really hurt, she is asking.

If he rushes to catch her out of gratitude,
guilt, self-loathing, obligation,
in effect he lets her fall.

. . . . .

Will it be now, or later?

Will it be now?

Will the moon burn over the tree-line

Will the arteries clutch

Will the brain in its shock-worn pockets smooth itself down

Being small, as we are, and negligible

Scarcely entitled to a name, such as *beloved*

Not known to exist except as *beloved*

As you were

Uncertain now what you are

Will the brick houses withstand the rest of winter

Will the wood houses

Will the men be warm enough at night

The women

Will each find his way to another, and be housed, and be free from harm

Will the man who sleeps under the plastic tarp under the bridge be free from harm

The families in the trailers

Will the bills ever ease

Will the tensions ease, slacken, and come to seem unimportant

Will you ever come to seem unimportant

Uncertain now who you are—

And when will this trance end?

Shapes night-wheeling in the breeze

Spurs of bone a patch of trees

Wind-washed and moon-fretted

A night composed of nothing

A herd of deer browsing on lichen

Train-horn pulling through the dark

Wing-splash

Killed in the wind farms

Tangled in the cell phone towers

The birds

The birds

The seed-heads loosening

The seed-heads loosening in bright-and-dull dawn.

. . . . .

Historically, all governments lie to their peoples.
Historically: bloodshed for trust.

The way a person lies is different
from the way a government lies.
Avert your eyes if you can.
You said it's MY DISEASE.

And that is true.

As my disguises were true.

Private fears my sense that you might not forgive.

People lie because they believe they can control outcomes.
They believe they know the way.

Today, am I in danger?

To what are you beholden?

By what enthralled?

If you understand, tell me

A war, a nation, oxblood and sleep kits.

When I wake up, I understand what slaughter will take place today in our name.

What should my response *be*

Who am I responsible *for*

What falsehoods count

And what men at this hour do not speak?

What women at this hour cannot speak?

Wind beneath the bridge, between the cemetery stones,
soundless. Last night's rain
shaking from the leaves.
Light pours down—

What is it that moves in such weather-
smooth winds that the hills themselves soften?
The pleats of snow in the ridges below the peaks
are cold. Depthless
beauty. I have not been able to say
I trust the world.

The war is with us each morning
With us when we climb into beds

When I wake up I am responsible
When I wake up alone, I am forced to see

Over the ossified earth the waters are rising
I avert my eyes

Each of us who has a home—
we darken

And the wonder of birds is that they still rise
The wonder of birds

I believe in what is gentle in us, despite what we have done

I believe I can praise everything I am not permitted to become

I believe there is no love in bluntness

But in the struggle toward attention

Which is light

You will never be alone

So that we *see* blades of grasses fog soaking the reeds

Raccoons dropping in pairs from the trees

And the burdens of others

Boys by the building hanging around without shoes

The clouds over rivers

Nightfall sweeps the globe

Rain-films of oil on asphalt

Crocus-bundles parking garages tickets plastic bags

You live despite disease

You thrive in understanding

A nightspray of deer on the hills

Snowy roads glowing with the boxed

Heat of travelers

Highways and overpasses

A crowded bus-stop someone shouting a finch

The supple swing of its voice laid over the air

As if we had closed our lips and eyes and felt

The cool stone inside us

Graphite and gold

Men exploding themselves in the streets

Women exploding themselves

Look—a bird is filling with light

Bracelets and mica bits

Greetings on the streets

I will help you although I do not know you

The raft of our efforts

Buoys in the bay

The myrtle flowers a few hour-boxed visitors

Senior citizens centers the impoverished schools traffic signs

That man hasn't eaten for days

Tonic and deadlock

Like the sun suspended in amber and flecked

With burnt wings, ancient civilizations of insects trapped in

Cold floating stone

Blotches of sky on my hands where I sense you

Wire fences invisible fences white clapboard steel gates

A few cottonwoods snowing down on the weeds

The ribs of a child an animal's

Sudden private cry

The raw sweep of the moon

And the water of looking

Tides pouring back

Trade-worn day-worn worn down by desires

And feel the winds move over the ruinous fields

Pesticides dispossession

A few blooms unnaturally early

Spring in February—

A death closes in.
Whose is it?

We need each other more.

NOTES

POETRY
Poetry

It left in the wind,
it returned in the air.

I opened wide
my door for it.

It left in the wind.
I woke to longing.

It left in the wind,
it returned in the air.

It carried me far
to a place of no one.

It left in the wind,
it stayed in my blood.

It returned in the air.

—José Ángel Valente, "La Poesía," translated by Robert Baker

WHAT IS (WAR)
"And the flesh will fall back into the earth, and the horror / into sweetness and the dark into the sun and the bees / thus born." —Susan Stewart's paraphrase of Virgil's *Georgics*, Book IV.281–314, in *Columbarium*

RAPTUS
"A blue door / opens in the wilderness" —Nick Gulig, "A Blue Door"

MY ENEMY
"Sudden raptus in the land, / arborescing." —Forrest Gander, "Escaped Trees of Lynchburg," *Science & Steepleflower*

"the way you hold a feeling" —Deb Busch, in conversation

HALF OMEN HALF HOPE

Restore to them what is no more present in them,
They will see again the harvest grain enclosed in the stalk and swaying
    on the grass.
Teach them, from the fall to the soaring, the twelve months of their face,
They will cherish their emptiness until their heart's next desire;
For nothing is shipwrecked or delights in ashes;
And for the one who can see the earth's fruitful end,
Failure is of no moment, even if all is lost.

—René Char, "Redonnez-leur…" *Selected Poems*, translated by Mary Ann Caws

"Like when your body first feels a season come…" —Laura Dunn, "Toward Newport"

AERIAL

"the spiraling glitters of pelicans above the cone marsh" —Judith Klink, in a letter

WONDER OF BIRDS

"I will give my hands hopelessly" —Matt Kaler, "To a Whitetail Found Brimming with Stars," *Neo* 8

Peter Tannenbaum

Joanna Klink is the author of two books of poetry, *They Are Sleeping* and *Circadian*. Her work has appeared in *Chicago Review*, *Boston Review*, and other journals. She is teaching at Harvard University.

PENGUIN POETS